ALSO BY EOGHAN MAC CORMAIC

Pluid (Coiscéim 2021)

On the Blanket (An Fhuiseog 2022)

Macallaí Cillín (Coiscéim 2023)

Eoghan Mac Cormaic

The Pen Behind
The Wire

A Decade of Prison Poems

Greenisland Press

This edition 2023
Greenisland Press, Belfast
e-mail: info@greenislandpress.ie

An imprint of Elsinor Verlag (Elsinor Press), Coesfeld, Germany.
e-mail: info@elsinor.de
website: www.elsinor.de

Cover design: Sean Misteíl; Artwork: Alison Mac Cormaic
Printed: Germany

ISBN: 978-3-949573-03-3

To smugglers–
especially smugglers of words

'Poetry always breaks out, like scabies, in jail.'
– Joseph Campbell, *As I was among the Captives,*
Prison Diary 1922-1923

ACKNOWLEDGMENTS

My thanks to Gerry Kelly for reading through these poems and saying enough to encourage me to let others see them. I am indebted, again, to Danny Morrison for his time and advice in bringing this to completion with this Greenisland Press publication. I'm delighted that some comrades, friends and family have agreed to record some of the poems in this book and to make their interpretations available.

To all of these, *go raibh maith agaibh.* QR codes at the end of the book link to the recorded poems.

PREFACE

When I was released from prison in 1991 after fifteen years I stuffed my worldly possessions into a couple of large, brown paper binbags. Most of my clothes I had given away—a relatively simple task since we were restricted to a maximum of three items of any piece of clothing and one single coat. But packed into those brown bags was the fruit of years of writing. Yellow A4 and A5 prison notebooks bearing a huge assortment of short stories, a novel, crossword puzzles, lectures, newspaper articles, an eight language Celtic dictionary and poems. In Irish and in English.

Shortly after being released my mother produced from hiding another eight albums of smuggled prison comms and a diary which spanned several years, all written on toilet paper or on cigarette papers. She had patiently transcribed much of it and hid all of it in a safe house, as British Army and RUC raids continued even though I was in jail.

Those musings, scribblings, anecdotes and memories began a thirty-year hibernation which from time to time I would attempt to stir but often it would be too vast, too difficult to revisit old friends long since gone, prison wings echoing with voices of comrades I would not see again.

In recent times we have all become more reflective. In 2020 we learned how quickly society can change. Once more the notebooks and bundles and albums were re-opened and re-read and eventually I made an attempt to put some order on, and draw some meaning from, them all. This collection (and a separate collection in Irish, *Macalla Cillíní,* Coiscéim 2023) is the result and it mainly covers the years 1981-1991, the years after the blanket protest ended. I hope some of the writing here gives an insight, limited as poetry can, to the type of thoughts and dreams we had in the H-Blocks of Long Kesh.

Eoghan Mac Cormaic, June 2023

CONTENTS

LIFE IN THE WINGS

AN EYE ON THE WORLD OUTSIDE

BEYOND THE WALLS

AUDIO FILES

Gerry Adams, Christy Moore, Séanna Breathnach, Lachlan Whalen, Rosie McCorley, Barra Mac Giolla Dhuibh, Alison Mac Cormaic, James Doran, Jim Ward, Danny Morrison, Martina Anderson, Raymond McCartney, Vincent Higgins, Verena Commins, Rita Ann Higgins, Laurence McKeown, Liadán Nic Cormaic, Colm Scullion, Paul McFetridge, Máiréad Farrell and Eoin Ó Broin, Brendan McFarlane, Pat Sheehan, Ali Mac Aindreasa, Eoghan Mac Cormaic, Jenny Meegan, Malachaí Mac Cormaic, Toiréasa Ferris, Diarmuid de Faoite, Tony Doherty, Gerry Kelly, Mitchel McLaughlin, Sarah McLaughlin, Órlaith Mac Eoin Manus, Lucilita Bhreatnach, Eibhlín Nic Cormaic, Máiridh Nic Cormaic,

Building Trouble

Over the wall, beyond the nearest block
swung the jib end of the derrick.
Below it, almost out of sight from us
hung a girder, heavy, solid, thick -
the sort of magic wand from which a prison
is constructed. 'Take some hacksaw
to cut a hoor like that, wouldn't it?'
asked Joe, of no-one in particular.
The yellow arm arced slowly like a bird
with a taut worm trapped within its beak
ninety degrees it turned to lay its burden down
without a strain, or groan, or creak.
The steel rope retreated upwards to the limb,
the arc reversed, I turned to roll a smoke
having seen it all before. Building always building
at their endless prison. Paddy spoke:
'They're always building something,' my thoughts
'We've seen this place grow from fields to this.'
He waved an arm at the expanse of walls and tins.
'Keeps them off the streets, eh? What a place?'
'What was it like at the start, then Joe?'
'Like a field, filled with rubble.'
'And what was the first thing they built then?'
'What they're always building. Trouble.'

Easter 1982

Early in the morning, we rose and cleaned the cells
and hurried to the yard.
In other yards, and cells and jails, prisoners like us
were readying, that same morning
some standing, some sitting
and all around us, screws, watching.
At the given time I heard the command:
Fall-in! Parade! Attention!
and from every yard there came a single sound,
the sound of five hundred boots hitting the ground
and I imagined I could hear them all.

The Roll of Honour was read, proudly,
and this year I listened, hearing for the first time
Bobby, Frank and Raymond, Patsy, Joe,
Martin and Kevin, Kieran, Tom and Mickey.
I remembered then, in that yard
in the quietness of Long Kesh, Easter 1982
I remembered another Easter, two years before
when we stood, with the Ten
behind our locked doors.
Naked but for our robes, our blankets. On protest.
Who thought, that day, that we would lose ten comrades
on hunger strike, demanding rights that now were greater
than clothes? And two years on
who could say the hungers strikers did not win?
Two minutes of silence. Parade! Dismiss!
and for a moment I heard again the soft sound
of five hundred bare feet stamping on the floor.

*The hunger strike ended in October 1981 and for the next year we remained
on a strike against prison work. We were entitled to daily exercise in the yard,
however, and Easter 1982 would be our first opportunity to commemorate our
fallen comrades.*

Mackies' Men

Crows overhead.
Black squawks on their nightly flight
from some wood
or daytime feeding ground
to a nightly lodging
the whereabouts of either
is beyond me in more ways than one.
For I am fixed
on a spot below a flight path
which hasn't changed
in all these years.
Only time changes.
And the sprawling prison down below.
Tonight they pass
at seven o'clock, last month eight
next month maybe five.
Always they will pass
just before the fall of dark.

Mackies' Men, we used to call them.
Black-clad hordes, homeward bound
after a day's work.
Time changes.
There's less in Mackies now
while the murder of crows
grows bigger by the year.

The Mackies engineering works in West Belfast gave rise to blanket man
Finbarr McKenna naming the nightly flight of crows 'Mackies' Men'. Ten
months after his release Volunteer Finbarr McKenna died on active service on
2 May, 1987.

Vigil

The straw that broke the camel's back
was in a cup of coffee that he drank
at eight o'clock. Caffeine stimulated
all the thoughts he should have left
beside his rolled-up jeans and
roughly-folded shirt upon the chair
beside the bed.

His head was
full of all the better-to-forget-about
things he'd rather leave until
the morning after passive slumber.
Thinks he hears a radio a-playing
knows he hears a screw a-whistling;
left side, right side, blanket overhead
frustration-creased sheets below
his feet and rumpled pillow add
to the ticking, clicking, creaking
pipes which scatter sleep until
he tries counting sheep until
their bleating fills his ears, and still
sleep stays clear. The cooling cell
prevents him walking out his rage.
he twists and turns, on edge
before at last, unannounced and
unbeknown to himself the sleep
he justly sought defeats the caffeine.
Lights go out and body eases,
limbs relax and rhythmic wheezes
signify the nightly cycle at its close.

*The pooling of our resources in the wing meant that there was often a jar of
communal instant coffee to tempt fate just before being locked in the cells for
the twelve hours overnight.*

Point Number Three

Opened envelopes slipping through my door
containing letters from my friends
were welcome. Pity though, that all
their words and thoughts were second hand
or second read before they reached me
indirectly through the censor's scanning,
prying, noting, blacking pen:
separating ignorance
from knowledge; the right to know
or have the knowing banned
for reasons of good order, discipline,
security or other such demands
on his discretionary power. Vis:
'Your cousin, *dark score,* called today.
He's moving house to *blank, blank*
next week and said to say
your old pal *blotch of ink* has hit
the drink and was in court
fined *something* pounds, pity, with
a wife and *smudge* children to support.'
And rightly so for why should I
be privy to such shattering facts
of social change and ripe disorder
that I might otherwise attack,
attempt to overthrow this solemn tranquil peace.
There's only Letter Censor Point Number Three
to act as guardian of stability
between the outside world and me.

Multitone Monotone

Nights are worse, I suppose,
on balance as the tinkle of
the mandolin like some honky
tonk piano on the higher notes
gives an unsolicited, unsteady,
planxty, jigging into reels
and untried rhythmic beats
O'Carolan never intended
while a trembling, treble whistle
fills the interludes in a minor
repertoire of three abysmal, dismal
tunes. 'Long time picking it up'
he'll admit tomorrow morning
as he does each day in apology.
I could pick it up at night
and twist it out of shape if
I was less the patient type
who knows how long it took to build Rome
and radios. Twenty comrades,
twenty stations all competing
with my own, the twenty first
adding to the tortuous tone
which seems to be the backdrop
every time the door is locked.
You could almost tour Europe via
twenty cells, a hectic tour at
a frantic pace on a decibel plane
and wistfully for all its beauty
I'd make it whistle stop.

The restoration of 'privileges' meant we were allowed transistor radios. The days of silence were over, and not always for the best.

Yardsticks

'The time was,' Jimmy said,
'When you could have bought a pint
for the price of a bar of chocolate,'
and four heads nodded,
couldn't argue for they'd heard
the argument that often
they could nearly tell before
he spoke the words that he would say.
Except Mick, who was newly down
- said himself he thought
he would have walked, but
Diplock thought differently
and sent him to the Blocks.
And new down, he hadn't heard
Jimmy's favourite gripe
about inflation from the good old days
of fifteen years before
when pints were standards
of the current rate of trade
at twenty pence or thereabouts.
And maybe so, he said, that
pints were cheaper then than
bars of chocolate today, but mind
the chocolate was bigger then for
half the price, so what, I ask you
have we gained and lost?
Heads nodded, knowing Mick had gained
so very little by his point but Jimmy
had lost his last fond memory of a golden past.

Closure

The hailstones were
coming down and in
at every angle
through the window.
I hated them doubly,
wanting to read a dry book
I had to rise
and shut them out.
Gains and losses
the cell stuffy now
without the breeze
to chase away my pipe smoke
and the bigger loss
to miss the sound of nature
touching down
beating the ground
chaos replaced by calm
freedom diminished
when you close yourself in
you're finished.

A Night Sound and a Thought

For all their locks and bars and doors
and chains and keys and polished floors
and rules to quote from well-thumbed books
and keys and chains and nonsensical looks
and lights and wire and walls and bricks
and searching hands and sneaking kicks
and visiting boxes in crowded rooms
and pipes that fail to warm these tombs
and censored letters and tasteless food
and governors, aggressive and rude
and boards for beds and beds for chairs
and cells that echo when lying bare
and disrupted sleep and distorted nights
and tins which block and bar out light
and day-in, day-out routine chores
and missing needs from plundered stores
and the ever-present watching screw
and the camera watching him watching you
and the lack of colour and the length of time
and the lie that what we've done is crime
is all for naught as if not there
when tonight at ten through the clear night air
came the sound of a horn from an ice cream van
and the laughter of a child who behind it ran
and I know not how the tinkling came
through walls and wire but it came, it came
and for all I've written it was clear to be seen
just how deep the loss of freedom has been.

The Eighth of the Eighth, Eighty-eight

Still in bed by the eight o'clock news
though wakened by the gate which spewed
forth the breakfast lorry
and that day's complement of screws.
Unlocked by twenty past
to fill the tea-urn, dilute six pints of milk
to produce three gallons, economics of
the community which by ten to nine was up and
working. Clean out today, washing walls
scrubbing sinks, gouging gutters, drying dishes,
lifting litter; a clean out is a communal action,
every mother's son is in a team of eight or
thereabouts
but these teams were shrinking
a final act, a parting gesture as two leave
today and two follow tomorrow to the other place
Maghaberry, with its options.
Exit four from here, exit forty-four from
round the camp, a varied group who yesterday
were part of us, and now, apart from us, depart.
Friendships pulling, bonds are strong but
the same bonds are pulling other bonds apart.
We're stronger yet we'll miss some, not all
for not all were part of what we are.
By dinner time it's one down, by tea-time two,
news of casualties in Ardoyne, news of truces
in Angola and the Gulf. Every war has
its own gulf to cross, ours has many.
By eight o'clock the gaps of departees
have been infilled and the final communal
actions of the day, fill the urn, empty the
dregs of the watery milk.
Tomorrow sees it all again.

*In 1988 some disagreements in the H-Blocks led to a small group of prisoners,
former blanket men, leaving the wings and attempting to set up an alternative
structure in Maghaberry Prison.*

Acquaintance Renewed

Walking up the wing tonight
I saw a face I hadn't seen in years—
ten years almost, less a month or two
and the face had changed. Older
and the silver shade of age on the hair
and crow's feet stamping years on the fold
at the side of the eyes, marking time.
They hadn't changed, still staring,
watching, a bit less assured maybe
and that pouting lower lip, like a bed
hanging out of a window, gave him away.
I mind him younger, at forty, a bull
of a man standing over my naked frame.
I was eight stone ten, he half as much again
and clothes, and boots, and other screws
to help him drag me from my cell.
He tried, I mind, to break my shoulder
with the door frame. Shoulders break easier
than conviction—and dignity weighs less
than all the clothes he wore. The bastard
tried and failed that day but he hurt me
all the same. Saw him eyeing me tonight
but I wouldn't give him the satisfaction
of recognition. Funny how his kind seem
to think we're almost old comrades,
the blanket screw and the blanket man, the
link being their infliction of what we endured.
Symbiotic. Know now how survivors
of Auschwitz feel when old ghosts come into view.

First published in Voices of Conscience. *Editors:* Cronyn, McKane, Watts, Iron Press, 1995.

Paul 'Beaver' Nugent 11.8.1988

He was twenty-two, a youngster in a wing
of men the most of whom had spent the half
of that in prison and had learned the ropes
learned how to size a situation up or put
a crisis down; learned how to take each new day
as it comes and leave as much of yesterday's
cares where they belong. In the past. He was
twenty-two and fighting fit but worried
that the health he cherished was dying on his
nimble feet. He shadow-boxed as was his wont
in the yard, ran a few miles in laps
alternating fast and slow, like his young heart
which he could hear thudding, pumping
crashing the life blood of his body round the
arteries and veins to nourish muscles some of us
had yet to find and the thrust of cardiac muscles
sounded a note of alarm in his raw mind
and panic, hectic, frantic panic at this new and
unknown sense of surging life. Bells of alarm
replaced the bells he used to fondly recall from the
boxing rounds he'd fought and won. Never out for
the count he now began to count the pulsing of his
heart, till that encircling tension shot up the beat
and in fear he asked advice. From the cell next door
a friendly calm voice would talk, and help him to relax
from the heights of frenzy to the steadiness of his own
two feet. We asked, knowing of his problem, for
the system to behave with just a little human grace
and let the sick one spend a few nights in the care
of the concerned one who we knew could help.
A simple uncomplicated move, we pointed out
the dangers, we pointed till we wearied, failed
to convince and disappointed for the boy who now
was ill, depressed, exhausted, listless already
only four weeks since the cycle began he was lost.
The new man, the sick and hopeless man had won the round
against the Kid and we, in his corner
reassured him, coaxed and primed him for

the days ahead. He rallied. He rallied for a day
or less and suddenly he slumped. It seemed as if
all hope had left him and he left us bewildered
wondering what it was that seeps into the mind
in such a rapid way to rob a rich full life
with everything in store to leave a plundered mind
that says no more, no more, and in four short
weeks takes a fighting spirit from the body
in exchange for black despair. Four weeks.
We got the news, we who tried to help. We who knew
the ropes were told he'd learned the ropes his own
way, had taken a dive, had been beaten on the ropes
had choked himself to death and we choked in grief,
we who thought we knew him and we mourned him
and we cursed the heartless system for its bureaucratic
rules. He killed himself and they drove him to it
and we ringside spectators, dumbly looking on.

*By the mid-1980s we took a decision to allow onto our wings some non-political
prisoners from nationalist backgrounds (doing short sentences for what we
termed anti-community behaviour). We reasoned that by experiencing our
politics they might be diverted from petty crime and adopt more productive
roles on their release. Some of these young people came from republican
families and were also victims of the conflict and social upheaval. Paul Nugent,
whose tragic, unnecessary death in prison inspired these lines deserved better
and for a short while in our wings he had better.*

A Dog's Life

Watching the dogs from below the tins
I lay, belly down on the damp ground.
A dozen dogs, a dozen handlers
the beasts straining at the leash
eager to follow the helmeted master
baton drawn, padded and shielded
into the manufactured fray.
The dogs, Alsatians for the most part
are the savage image of their masters
and if dogs could be so trained
they'd bark out bigotry
with tails wagging in furious glee.
They say that dogs like these
are trained to obey but one master
and if the master dies, the dog is shot.
Workers trained to one trade
and if that trade dies, the worker starves.
The same use value for dog and worker
both are expendable, both are tools.
I watch the dogs being led away
as the riot squad withdraws
angry, disappointed, unsated.
Man's best friend and our worst enemy.
Even if we had peace and justice
We'd have to put them down.
You can't teach an old dog new tricks
and while swords can make ploughshares
these dogs are beyond the pale.

No News, Good News

Like monks in a monastery
long cut off from an outside life
and facing inwards to their daily grind
we prisoners walk the yard
swopping worn out, tired old tales:
tales we've all heard before
but, too polite to interrupt
we listen again, laughing on cue
repeating the punchline as if in awe
while the teller slaps his thigh
as if in the pleasure of the first telling.
And new arrivals listen
enjoying for the first time
a yarn that took a hundred tellings to perfect.
Dutifully, in turn, they reply:
their first story, a premier,
unrehearsed it wins warm applause
because it's new.
Next day, next week, next year
the story will be re-polished,
rephrased, re-used, revised
until it too becomes a part
of the stale stock of stories we share
like monks in a monastery
long cut off from an outside life
and facing inwards on our daily grind.

The Ghosts of Armagh Gaol

For almost three years now within Armagh Gaol
Irish women have suffered untold pain
no other country would allow this sorry shameful tale
of strip searching, Britain stands accused again.

The women most vulnerable are those still on remand
attending court on most days of the year
They say it is intolerable and make just one demand
Stop the strip and end the days of fear

Their protests go unheeded as all clothing is removed
to allow a full 'inspection' by the screws
the British say it's needed yet nothing has been found
brutality is the price if they refuse

There are people more concerned today with the rape of
Emain Macha
with its limestone quarry, eating up the past
while not so many miles away in the prison of Ard Mhacha
there's a rape in progress as each day goes past.

In Maghaberry and in Brixton Irish women pay the cost
of standing firm behind the Irish race
and as they finally shut the locks on Armagh and its ghosts
Strip searching will be its last disgrace.

Senses

Where the senses fail us
is when the senses act alone
we need them together
a co-operation of detectors
to guide our perception.
The crackle of a log fire
can be heard but heat must be felt.
The smell of flowers may
be sprayed from a can, so touch
is needed to be sure
and sight must work with taste
before we'll know if the fruit is bitter.

Stroller

Stroller. Music spilling from
the ever-present radio
hooked at the wrist
hooked in the mind
steps in rhythm to a beat
that changes song to song.
Crackles on the corners
trebles on the straight
dull bass on the crossing
near the gate. The songs vary
with the passing minutes
interspersed with waffle
no one hears or listens to
waiting only for the *Musak*
killing time as if walking
was a lonely task best performed
to the beat of a new drum
of hits and blues and rock
around the block from now
till noon, untangle the
thong and wait for another
stroll and roll at two o'clock.

The Republican Writer's Test

And Bobby Sands's most famous lines
become *da-da, dee dee.*
In this, the very block where he wrote those lines
here in the dreaded H-Block 3.
Where ten years back in *pluid* proud
he stood on cold feet, by the door
to sing a song for Derry men, of a city fair
United men would see no more.
Who around him then could dare to think
that song would make the *Ra Ra* repertoire
for drunken patriotic balladeers to sing
when alcoholic seeds had flowered
on nights like this when a rag tag band
minds muddied by homebrewed wine
would make the words come tumbling out
so only *da da dee dee* fits the rhyme.
The signal I suppose, that Bobby's made it big
is that he now is lilted like the rest—
Moore, Kickham, Behan and their half-known songs:
Bob's missing lines enshrine him with the best.

While on the blanket Bobby Sands wrote a poem The Voyage *which was also sang to the air of* The Wreck of the Edward Fitzgerald *by Gordon Lightfoot. Christy Moore adapted it, adding a bridging chorus – 'I wish I was back home in Derry'. The song* Back Home In Derry *has now become a famous anthem and has been recorded multiple times by musicians around the world. It is about the deportation and gruelling transport of Irish rebels from Derry in 1803, exiled by England to Van Diemen's Land (Tasmania), pining for their wives and children and the town and homeland they love.*

Easter 1989

Gathering of comrades
remembering
fallen friends,
our roots
those whose deaths
inspired others of us.
We listen
to names of young men,
young women,
poets
whose lines
marked the contours
of city streets
and country fields
and we read lines
in their memory
for we still have poets
to complete
their unfinished verses.

By the middle of the 1980s republican prisoners in the H-Blocks had begun commemorating their fallen comrades by way of an Easter pageant, with songs, drama, poetry and music.

Inhospitality

Just a cuff was enough
to bind me to the law
as I walked, closely stalked
by the six or eight I saw
running past, very fast
every opening we met
on the way to the X-ray
every face in stolid set.
People hurried as I studied
every step, and stone, and spot
on my travel to unravel
one uncertain stomach knot.
Those who saw me did not see me
for their eyes were turned away
from the rifles, friendship stifled
no one cared or dared to say
'Hello how are you? Good to see you,
How are things up in the jail?'
Pointed muzzles act as muzzles
eyes avert and all words fail
Until I saw there, on a wheelchair
one who could not be contained
and he smiled, and so defiled
all their guns and locks and chains.

A trip to an outside hospital was always an occasion of high drama, with armed police and armed soldiers running through hospital reception and A&E departments to ensure their prisoner would not escape.

Going Under

Too tired, too thick-tongued
to wonder as the needle made its sharp entry
I made a sharper exit
from alert
to inert

It is the shock
of waking in a different bed
dressed in different clothes
surrounded by different walls
hearing different voices
that makes the mark
that shakes belief
that underlines
just how unconscious I have been.

Check. For the plaster on the hand
and the tape on the forearm.
Check. The exact time now
and the approximate time then.
Check. The limbs, the joints
the eyes, the voice.
As I check, they check
imponderables I do not understand:
blood pressure, temperature, all neatly logged
as I half doze
climbing from the haze
is a slower process
than going under.

Years after the blanket protest some prisoners still required hospital visits to treat ailments dating back to the protest conditions.

The First Official Language

'I can't tell you how strange I feel,' he wrote
'talking to you here in English.'
Strange times we're living in, I thought
and read on 'if you get my gist,
I don't know you in English.' And he was right.
For there, behind the walls of Long Kesh
we had met and the Irish we were taught
was the language we'd converse:
go dtí an deireadh Béarla was remote
and yet we were no less able
to relate, communicate
and learn. Until last week—release
cast him back upon an English-speaking world. Mate
or cara that he was and is
he sent a letter. The censor denigrates
the use of the *Teanga Dhúchais*
so future contact now necessitates
re-learning to communicate. In English.

This is a poem I wrote about a letter from Marcas Mac Ruairí. Twenty years later we would end up working together and would continue as work colleagues and friends for almost eighteen years beyond that. As Gaeilge!

go dtí an deireadh: until the end
Béarla: English language
Teanga Dhúchais: native language

Mental Playground

In a night of boredom
long after the curtains had been pulled
long after the last motorway sounds
of returning travellers had lulled
I lay awake.
I lay, and then I wandered
to the toy box and playground of my mind
and opened dusty boxes
to see what entertainment I could find
to while away the hours.
Strange toys and games indeed.
Memory: thinking, imagination,
planning, guessing
composing and contemplating.
And wishes.
Memory: the swirling of a helter-skelter.
Thinking: the ups and downs of a seesaw.
Imagination: the roundabout of passing scenes.
Guessing: just a game.
Composing, on a canvas of the mind.
Contemplating: hiding and seeking out.
And the favourite toy, wishes,
gently rocking like a swing boat.
And I'm asleep.

Election Build-up

We were building up. Odd term that
for an ideal, a mood, a notion.
We were building for months, then weeks
and finally days. Preparing with a light
tool-kit of words, gestures, a look
a nod; easy-to-carry implements
that needed no packing when the time
we'd been building for arrived. And then
instead of building up we were counting down
and using different tools to analyse
and criticise and organise. Soon
we'd know if what we'd built fulfilled
the architecture that was planned.

Language and Pain

What do you write
when a comrade suffers loss?
What words can soothe, what phrase
will ease the pain?
What are words anyway? A means
of communication, an expression,
a thought, a gesture, a feeling
voiced. But words are spoken
and this feeling I want to denote
is in the heart not the mind.
Words are impersonal, words
are the common property of all;
feelings of the heart are personal
private, human to human.
What words will ease your pain, comrade?
What words will lift the burden
of death? No words. I shouldn't
even write. I should reach out
and hug you, shake your hand,
let your sorrow rest on my shoulder
but I can't. You're far away
in another cell and I am here,
pen-poised, trying to put a human
gesture into words. Words don't
fail me. Words simply fail to
fill the gap between hearts
and the lexicon of bodies
can't be written down.

A Reflection Across the Yard

Across the yard from this wing
sits an identical row of cells
It's occupied by loyalists
and some will say they can tell
the difference by the windows
–ours are sparse and bare.
Theirs are lined with personal goods
while over here—we share.

We don't have much in common
It's always them and us
we rarely meet and seldom talk
we've nothing to discuss.
And looking out our windows
both sides are framed in bars
but they see Taigs and we see Huns
and neither side see the stars.

At night when all the cells are lit
and I stand up by the door
I can look across and see them
like they see me I'm sure.
And times I wonder what they think
when they look across and see.
Do we ever cross their minds at all?
What do they think of me?

First published in Voices of Conscience. *Editors:* Cronyn, McKane, Watts, Iron Press, 1995.

Unity

We is a plural word denoting single.
We is the word which best describes a wing.
We act. We live. We think in union.
We, though many, are one. *In pluribus unum.*

A problem arises, the wing is informed
the meeting is organised
we come together we pool our views
on action we decide.
All thoughts collected and statements probed
all ideas put to the test
this is the dialectic at work
and it's now we are working best.
The problem is framed then torn apart
to analyse its cause
And once broken down to constituent parts
we examine each for flaws.
Each aspect is solved in a double way
in isolation and as part of the whole
Each comrade is free and welcome to talk
and many fulfil the role.
When all who wish to speak have spoken
the problem is reframed
now all understand the issue in full
and options are assessed again.
A consensus view is drawn together
a decision collectively made
with the agreement and adherence of all
unity is again displayed.

Reflection

The glint of light on a sole grey hair
caught my eye today.
One filament of protest
barging out its loneliness
on a balding pate.
There was a time when I
would have shuddered
at the thought of a silver thread
appearing on my dark head.
Now, instead, I welcome it
glad to find one
that has chosen to resist
instead of falling out.
A strand of steel among rushes.

My Gain, Your Loss

Neighbouring windows
of neighbouring cells
looking out on the same yard
and watching the same bird
feeding on shared crumbs
the two of us supplied.
Your bait was thrown
to bring a sparrow
mine, for any bird.
Your pleasure is in viewing
the beauty of the living thing
being tamed.
I tap the window
the bird flies off.
My gain, your loss
my pleasure is in the living thing
exercising its freedom.

Ground Level

The sound of the last pair of boots
to jump from the jeep was heard
at the same time as the first boot
smashed through the door.
A dozen pairs of boots
marched into the hallway:
four to the dingy living room,
four to the kitchen and backyard
and four that ran up the stairs
echoing on bare boards which creaked.

A pair of bare feet
stepped from the bed and toes
searched and found
a pair of worn slippers below it.
The slippers padded to the room door
which splintered as that first boot,
a practiced boot, struck it open
forcing the slippers to retreat in shock.
In another room a pair of runners
was being carried between finger and thumb
and tip-toes took them to the window
which glided open, and the runners
dropped quickly and quietly
on to a coal shed roof. Hurriedly
they were tied in place to the escaping feet.
The boots trampled over disrupted furniture
kicking, gouging, dismissing
tracing and re-tracing steps.
On a street corner a boot softly crushed
the red end of a cigarette into the ground
and slunk back
into the blackness of a doorway
at the sound of the approaching runners,
but with practiced timing

one boot shot forward
to trip between the runner and the ground
and another boot crashed quickly
into the ribcage of the unconscious figure.
Twelve pairs of boots stopped
as a radio crackled 'prisoner taken'.
The slippers folded, heel up, in prayer
as the boots made a noisy exit
which almost muffled a shot
from further up the street.

The expensive leather shine
of the shoes was perpetuated
by the swish of the black soutane
which brushed mud from the toes.
On the broken soil beside the hole
the shoes looked out of place
as they stepped back from the grave
into the ranks of brogues, stompers,
high heels, platforms, Docs
and trainers. The muddied shoes
pressed spades into the mound
and began to fill the deep hole
as six pairs of identical black shoes
came to attention, left down beside right
dismissed and mingled with the masses
in solid step past the ranks
of heavy black boots beyond the gates.

The soft sensible shoes squeaked
slightly, pivoting from heel to toe
in legal pose, while in the witness box
removed now from the tripping boots
uncomfortable sweating feet
in unaccustomed brown suede
marked figures of eight
into the carpet as the lies unfolded.
At each adjournment a dozen pairs of mixed shoes,
carefully picked shoes
would exit left, to the jury room

not one out of step.
Each night, sitting by a lonely fire
a pair of fur boots would be exchanged
for the old slippers.
The ritual continued for a week
and then, one unexpected day
at tea-time, weeks into the adjournment
they tensed, hard pressed
into the battered linoleum
as the radio crackled:
'Prisoner resisted says jury.'
One slipper stamped the ground in frustrated rage
and then resumed the lonely pacing.

Reflections on the British Army and RUC's 'shoot to kill' policy and cover-ups by the courts.

Reading Between the Lines in Gibraltar

I believe, Sir, that they, Farrell, McCann, and Savage
the deceased
might have had a button or a gun and
were
intent to murder. Our action that day was
legitimate
not part of any secret plan to kill
targets
although these people were well-known terrorists
who
we knew were trained and dangerous
we killed
but we used minimum and reasonable force
one
could of course have used more
after
the warning we gave, or perhaps didn't give led
the other
to the sequence of events and
to satisfy
the public safety of
the
Gibraltar citizens, indeed
British
lives were under threat. The evil
desire
of the bombers was well known
for
detonating remote control bombs in
revenge
attacks. We believed it was a button
we
believed fully and we fired a legitimate
shot
twenty-seven shots and killed, I can remember seeing
them without
a bomb, it wasn't there but they pretended to move
any

one could have thought it was aggressive. My
warning
shout was unintelligible I suppose
and
like a scream, it sounded like
this
Yaargh. I hadn't time for polite
examination
or civil requests. I suspected a button
job
was there, that they would push it
should
first opportunity arise, even though I
now
know the bomb wasn't there it was
clear
to me. They wanted to kill
everyone
in the vicinity, so in fact anyone
who
might have wanted to have a button brings,
serves
and gives notice on themselves. The question of whether
the
bombs existed is irrelevant though maybe
forces
an admission, it might not have been but
of
course, as a serving member of
the
security forces I know when a terrorist
British
bomber makes a move tries to overthrow
government
authority by sudden moves, I'll shoot
so
fast they'll be dead long before I
shut up
Take it from me, A, B, C and D will tell

you
the exact same story we know the
Irish
Republican Army think that we're murderous
bastards
they'll stop at nothing to subvert
Britannia
our British Justice, it's strong. The terrorist
waives
due process, the law. We always play by
the rules.

This verse was penned to show the doublespeak of the British legal system.
Three different stories emerge from the lines.

Biko

And the last sad lines
of a native son
were written across the page.
The parallel bars
of the colour guard
flanked the fallen from the rage.
The green and black
and golden flag
draped across the catafalque
as the dancing throng
of a people wronged
raised the dry red dust like talc
while an African beat
led the mourners' feet
to a stadium filled with pride,
to the conscious folk
of whom Biko spoke:
the people for whom he died.

In Chile, Allende,
In Ireland, Sands,
In South Africa Biko is slain
but their prophetic words
will be whispered and heard
Venceremos - We will rise again.

'It is better to die for an idea that will live, than to live for an idea that will die.'
– Steve Biko, 1946-1977

Mandelamandla

There he is now. There's Mr Mandela.
and zoom lenses brought you
through the heat and haze
and space of a hemisphere
past the stopped clock of Apartheid
through the unlocking prison gates
to the people.
Forward to the past,
the past returning to shape
the future. In focus
out of the prison you walked,
inside our TV, inside our canteen,
inside our prison, behind our locks.
Twenty-four comrades watched
your every step, Madiba.
Our ghetto is not Soweto
though we share your struggle.
Our prisons are still locked
though we share your liberation.

On the February day that Nelson Mandela walked free from prison people were transfixed as through the heat haze and dust walked a man who had spent twenty-seven years in jail. We were also glued to the television, that day, inspired by Mandela, many of us probably allowing a thought to flicker that one day we too might be released.

Funerals

In piercing ringing tones
the clergyman's voice called down
the wrath of God on
the perpetrators. 'Let them atone
by their blood. Yes, their own,
for Vengeance is Mine alone,'
saith the Lord: but let us postpone
the Lord's judgement until the Throne
and today let there be no groan
of anguish when the stone
is cast to strike down
the killing scum, the widow's moan
speaks louder to me. Root them out
and take them out of commission.

The young mother faced the camera light
face lined by a sleepless night
she spoke of her husband's fight
to survive, try as she might
she could not hold her emotions tight
and tears flowed, the sorry sight
of two children, eyes bright
innocent of the event or their plight
'I want no one to retaliate,'
she whispered. It seemed trite
to ask her how she felt, the slight
figure grasped her children
and turned and left the killing site.

The Face of Christ

Christ stared at me from a picture.
Bloodshot eyes, little wonder really
after a night in the cells and awaiting
His execution.
This was no sanitised *Ecce Homo*
with piety painted into the face.
Instead, Jesus had a shiner,
an early version of Castlereagh
or a Chilean stadium, or Winston Green
or Pollsmore Prison.
So, what's new?
The clergyman bemoans the dwindling flock
of faithful. Is Christ irrelevant? he asks
and I look at the battered face
the tangle of thorns, the early grey hair
on a thousand political prisoners.
Christ knows. He's not outdated.
He's daily emulated.

On My First Bike

A travelling man came through our street, my
Independence Day.
That's when I bought my first bike: big, old,
heavy, battle-grey.
And a bell of course, with a urgent clang:
look out! look out! it frantically rang.
It must have given service to someone else before
on quiet roads, car-free, carefree on bog, on hill,
on shore.
Its marks of age amused me, I loved its wear and
tear.
'How much for the Daisy Bell?' I asked. 'Give
me a price that's fair.'
I haggled, like a grown-up, he asked me for a
pound.
Ten shillings I gave, but really, it was worth but
half a crown.
He slipped me a shilling back for luck that 'the
better now, you'll feel,'
we spit on our palms and parted, a handshake
sealed the deal.

I wondered who rode it before me: traveller,
teacher, priest?
how many miles did it travel? North, South, West
or East?
The gypsies moved on that autumn day in
nineteen sixty-eight
as the bike and I began our journey along the
paths of fate.
That bike was the first thing I paid for with
money that was my own
a rite of passage from boy to man on a day that
seeds were sown.
October the fifth in Derry, news reached us in
hurried tones
from Duke Street, police attacks, water cannon,
broken bones.

I cycled the wind to view the scene, the RUC,
ominous, black,
batons still at the ready, there was no turning
back.
Two rites of passage on one day: childhood at a
close.
Our playground now a battlefield from injustice
struggle grows.
I turned the bike for higher ground and peddled
up like hell
and warned my friends of danger and rang that
frantic bell.

Fringe life

Keeping company with the scavenging gulls
and no-longer nervous rats
I scanned the dump site
home of the huddled masses
survival amidst despair
Beyond the tip, tombs
of the last instant culture
humanity's bleak and putrid headstone
a level plain
of cast-off waste
and grim foraging children.
Pungent tangent
to the city of the rich
its skyscrapers a palisade
to fence out the rejected
their suburbs,
overconsumption
the only link
between the good life and the poverty
that the Foster Grant and Polaroid-protected
eyes will never see.

I wrote Fringe Life *after reading about the favelas (shanty towns) in Brazil.
Open University courses gave many prisoners insights into life and struggles
across the world to add to the breadth of our wing, political libraries. But, more
importantly, OU lecturers gave encouragement to think and question in a
prison system (which discouraged thinking and questioning).*

Teacher

Sometimes, on your way to the jail
you might pick up a bright pebble in the park
or a seed pod windblown in the dark
of an autumn morning.
The urge to bring something new
to the drab grey H-Block class,
smuggling behind your prison pass
innocuous little things.
Books were never going to be enough:
education was not to be confined,
seek all and every source to feed the mind
there's knowledge in every single thing.

Cnoc na gCróga

Just a mile from Killypeadar on the road to
Monadoo
Where the stream from Cnoc na gCróga meets
the path,
you can see across the hillside a barren patch of
ground
that signals clear some old invader's path.
For the ground shows signs of scorching and
stonework thrown askew
on a site where once a humble cottage stood
but the spot is long deserted now, there's not a
single sound
to commemorate the homestead and its brood.
Was it violence that wiped away this humble Irish
farm?
Did some enemy come raiding in the night?
Did the mountain hear the battle sounds of
crashing sharpened steel?
and cries of terror coming from the fight?
Did Cnoc na gCróga see the family rising in
alarm?
Did she tremble when they finally lost the day?
Did she hang her head in mourning, anguish for
the family feel
while her streamlets washed the bloody stains
away?
Or did some tragedy occur that destroyed this
Irish clann?
Did the fire spark and set alight the thatch?
Did the father sense the danger to his family's
precious lives
Did the danger grow too great for him to match?
Did the mountain watch in horror as the flames
consumed the man
who fought to save his children from their doom?
Did the blaze engulf them all leaving not one to
survive?

Did the charred earth act as bier and shroud and
tomb?
But no, 'twas not these reasons but a hunger long
and fierce
that laid this Irish family in their grave
though brave they stood and starved among their
rotting crops
the peasants died so the landlords could be saved.
Yes the mountain heard the crying, the sound its
soul did pierce
on the cursed day that brought the bailiff's flame.
Too weak to fight they stood and watched and did
not raise a hand
then the mountain waters washed away their
shame.
Hunted from their dwelling place by the
landlord's flaming spleen
in the bare unsheltered ditches they'd be found
while England's lords and ladies dined and
laughed their cares away
Irish peasants starved below the ground.
And a mile from Killypeadar there's a headstone
to be seen
Half-buried now and worn smooth with age
and it marks just one of many spots where Gael
was made to pay
in the Famine years, our history's darkest page.

August 1979

The Year of the Frog

This is the Year of the Frog, said she
and she laughed, *ha ha* and she laughed *hee hee*
and a wizened old hag of a woman was she
and she sneered and leered and jeered at me
and clasped her hands for the business you see
more work, said she, for the old *bean sí*
as she pointed a warty old finger at me
and gasped for air and said, you'll see
The Year of the Frog is here, said she
and she twittered and tittered and flittered with glee
we're all getting blown to eternity
and a mushroom cloud was plain to see
and death held its breath for a moment or three
and the horrible hag climbed up a tree
but the tree caught fire and so did she
and nothing escaped on land or sea
but the mushroom grew in the air and we
were sorry we didn't die or flee
but the witch said, where would you go, *hee hee*
to escape your share of the agony
and she said, Croak 'n' Die, Croak 'n' Die, said she
don't you know it's the Year of the Frog, said she
so we all croaked together. RIP. DV.

The Last Protesting Voice

When the only sounds of protest
the only words of a prisoner to be heard
are the choking, gasping,
strangled, death-rattling creaks of a suicide,
something is wrong.

Wrong? In Mountjoy
they would not let her
hold her baby on a visit.
No joy in The Joy
except the sheet-made rope.

In Long Kesh they would not
let him share a cell
nor share his frantic thoughts
with a sympathetic ear
and only the torn-to-strips
comforter brought comfort.

In P4W in Kingston
the women have privileges to lose
in segregation units the only privilege they keep
is in the sheet and choice
of time of death announced in strangled voice.

Your system, in Ireland,
in Canada, in Australia
in every dark prison hole
is the same. A killer.
A muffling wall which smothers
and only lets the final sound be heard.

P4W was a women's prison in Kingston, Ontario, where in the late 1980s seven inmates died by suicide.

Ashes

Peace floated on the Ganges
and a dream, an ideal, lay in ashes
when Gandhi died.

Courage was bleached in quicklime
and a dream, an ideal lay in ashes
when the GPO fell.

Strength withered in rotting fields
and a dream, an ideal, lay in ashes
when a peasant cottage burned.

Wisdom singularly failed
and a dream, an ideal, lay in ashes
below the napalm flames.

Hope smouldered, almost smothered
and a dream, an ideal, lay in ashes
while a Phoenix sought peace,
courage, strength, wisdom
for the life that was to come.

Marchers

Behind a banner
the crowd is disorderly, orderly
in the photograph.
The older experienced veterans
fewer now, among the young.
A face turned sideways in conversation
a downward glance at a carried wreath
a heavy coat, a head scarf; plain people,
a camera slung around a neck
idly, hopefully idle
and capturing no more
than this reconvened mass
of the faithful who have walked
sadly, proudly, defiantly
along this route. Seventeen Sundays,
seventeen years, and the offspring
the children who weren't born
when that first march
made cameras click in shocked horror
as fourteen fathers, brothers, sons
were slain
and thousands survived the ambush
on these streets
remembered today, and always
by the marchers.

This poem, published in Harrowing of the Heart, *is a tribute to all those who marched for justice, year after year, for the victims of Bloody Sunday.*

Reluctant Appreciation

Soft pink hands, I mocked
that had never known hard work
unlike the craftsman's hands, hard
from cutting wood, ebony, ivory,
shaping this. I listened, seeing
the proud fulfilment of his tool
as pink hands in white gloves
played, making music, on his piano.

A Donegal Shepherd to his Sheep

That wind that's blowing up white foam
on the sea, a hundred feet below you, sheep
curling like your horns round a rock
and coming all the way from Tory
tells me it's winter. Tory is lost,
wrapped in a grey mist. You, sheep,
will soon be mutton and I will be
wrapped in your thick coat.
In this wind I need it more than you.

The Party Worker

You are the backbone of the struggle, comrade
solid in purpose, straight in strategy
flexible in tactics.
You lift with the strength of our thousand muscles.

You are the mist of the struggle, comrade
your work is unseen in its approach
but like the mist we feel a moist effect
the dew you deposit before moving on.

You are the patience of the struggle, comrade
success you take equally with setback
you build on success
and stoically learn from failure.

You are the experience of the struggle, comrade
the wise builder who selects tools and stone
we are the tenants of your work
the inheritors of your organisation.

Camilo Torres

Fine gentle hands
marked him out from the rest:
Before this their only use
was in celebrating mass
for his people
dressed in vestments
of liturgical colours.
Until that day during the sacrifice
when turning
bread to flesh and wine
to blood,
knowledge struck him
like a rifle butt
and he left his vestry
in rough combat colours
shaking at the thought of his future
walking through shanty slums
towards the hills
towards the ultimate vocation
the change from servility
to struggle
and only when he took off his cassock
did he finally become a priest.

Fr Camilo Torres from Bogota broke with the Church hierarchy and actively took part in the struggle for freedom, against injustice, corruption and inequality in Colombia. In 1965 he joined the ELN (National Liberation Army), a guerrilla army based in the mountains that had been inspired by the Cuban Revolution. He was killed in action in February 1966 and was mourned by thousands of peasants who put up flowers and crosses in his honour.

Creggan Hill

So this is where they finally buried you, cara
Here on this hillside overlooking the river
a hillside which journalists would call bleak
when describing a funeral
but would call sunbathed
if describing the ghetto housing
which straddles the brow above your plot.
Aye, you'd know that already old friend
that journalists and media folk
make scenes from chosen words
rather than words from chosen scenes
and their every word is laden
with a value to reflect for others
not what they see
but what they want to be seen;
not what they know
but what they want to be known.
It amazed me you know,
the variations they had for you.
Most just said, 'gunman buried'
but one or two described you ...
'the man with the killer's eyes'
and 'he didn't know how to laugh'
caught my eye. Killer's eyes indeed
and you didn't have much to laugh about
the way it was.
I saw it on TV; your burial.
A dishonoured guard of RUC
flanking the hearse. It was, I thought,
the closest they'd ever been to you.
One paper described it as a rabble funeral,
maybe they meant rebel, for you were
an old rebel at twenty, at twenty-five
on the run but safe among your own
and buried almost on the run.
The sun is warm on the field today
I see a few visitors around Cuchulainn.
It's a lonely spot I suppose

and on wet days, maybe bleak
like they said in the report
but only for visitors, you know
or maybe you don't but I'll tell you.
It's only the living who can be lonely
and only the living can know bleakness
and sometimes, I think,
the greatest loneliness
is in coming to a place like this
and knowing you're gone
and I'll never hear your voice,
see your face, touch your life again.

Written in memory of my friend and comrade Ciarán Fleming who escaped from the H-Blocks in September 1983 and was tragically killed in action on 2 December, 1984.

Gas

The cartridge spun on the ground,
smoke lay in a cloud.
It clung to the rain
which covered the streets,
it stung the eyes
and burned the nose.
We dipped rags in vinegar,
wrapped the rags around our faces
and turned to do battle again.

Beer

Bottles broke against the wall
with the sound of bells
and a tinkle.
We drank beer
and disposed of the evidence
by vomiting
and sucking Polo mints.
Youth was ringing in our ears.

The Mountain

Tall and grey, etched on a mountain of a clear blue sky
the mountain stands majestic over all
Lord and Master, the king and comforter of all
that lies around
where e'er his gaze might fall

See, now, kissed by the morning sun his skin is scored
by shadows, a tribute from the lonely pine trees
that he keeps
thriving and well, kept alive by his cool black soil
moistened by silver streams where small fish leap.

Small bubbling streams, making music where they meet
beneath his snowy cap, last winter's fall
ribbons of refreshment, carrying water along his length
to all his creatures great and small

Warmed by the sun throughout the day till evening
brings the moon, to o'er the mountain's shoulder peep
silhouetted now
in bulk and beauty,
God's gift to us the mountain sleeps.

The Divil

the day they took me into the fold
I cried like the baby I was I'm told
as over my head poured waters cold
to chase the divil away

the day I first sat down in school
to study, be taught and learn the rule
I sat there like an innocent fool
and gave my freedom away

the day I first began to toil
to earn my share of other people's spoil
I spilled my sweat to damp the spoil
that stole my strength away

the day I first saw steel-barred doors
I mourned for all that I'd lost before
no tears, no freedom, no strength no more
the divil returned to stay.

Grooks (after Piet Hein)

Optimist or pessimist
I'd always choose the latter
for the optimist has reached the best
while the other can only get better.

The art of putting into verse
some wisdom worth relating
is that the wisdom must be such
that it isn't worth debating.

Piet Hein was a Danish polymath whose short poems were known as gruks *or* grooks. *When the Nazis occupied Denmark he joined the Resistance.*

The Hunter and the Hunted

For my mother

If I look with such a jaundiced eye
at those who now my freedom run decry
don't think of me unsporting as I flee
a flash of russet fur 'neath knotted tree
and thorny bush or jagged tangled briar
and loll my tongue of pink and flick the fire-
coloured tail they call my brush
at unseen pesky flies, or if I blush
behind my soft red-haired and pointed snout
while in my ears I hear pursuers shout
and curse my luck, and urge the canine foe
to seek this foxy prey, and tally-ho
as horns sound and flutter in the breeze
in a short-lived truce I gasp and wheeze
and hunting dogs sniff out my latent trail
along invisible paths the hounds now sail
yapping, barking, leading, prowling, cursed dogs
over dale and ditch, round wood and bog
I run scurry, lope and hurry, cunning is my forte
and I must now outwit this devilish sport
I seek and draw the pack towards a bank
and swerve and run towards the hunter's flank
while yelping baying pups increase their pace
and foolishly believe I've lost the race
In leaps and jumps they clamour for my skin
of foxy fur, but danger lies within
an easy-looking win, I see my prey
brown, black and white and dapple grey
equine hunters, saddled masters stunned
to see the wily fox towards them run
and snapping at his heels a surly pack
of growling hounds who can't draw back
as into the horses' hooves they charge
while cunningly, this fox remains at large

August 1982

69

Home on Friday

Ten minutes into my own elation
at the news
you sat down, anticipation
as if you knew
to ask me, what's the situation?
And I told you
home on Friday
thirteen years of separation
were through
in your tightening hug
and exclamation
long overdue
and this weekend a celebration
it's true

Home on Friday

One Tuesday morning in August 1989 while waiting in the circle area of the block to go on a visit I was suddenly informed that I was to be released for three days parole on the Friday. Try receiving that news with sangfroid!

Competing Perspectives

'Any medical complaints?'
completed the formalities
and as I shook my head the MO
muttered that 'McCormick
has just started the slippery slope
to release.'
Only the keeper
could use that phrase.
The kept, me,
I would see it as the start
of an uphill climb
to freedom, upwards and outwards
from their dark pit.

MO: Medical Officer, a medical is required as a pre-release formality.

Through the Turnstile

'Take a deep breath,' somebody, maybe Dan, was calling
and, smothered in arms, choking on relief
I needed that breath.
Behind me,
as the turnstile clicked out another comrade,
forward and out, trickles of freedom
into the roar and rush
of a hundred flushed, happy faces.
I breathed deeply, counting the clann
of father, mother, sister, brothers, aunts,
sisters-in-law to an outlaw, nephews, nieces
into a wave and push away from the gate.
Five past ten, Friday the twenty fifth of August
all I wanted was road signs
speeding past and taking me to Derry,
taking me home.
Eyes focussing, tears welling, memories flooding back
and all around me like a protective shield
my family. *Ár Lá Tagtha.*
Mind, body, morale, family intact.
Buíochas le Dia.
We're on the road.

Ár Lá Tagtha: Our day had come.
Buíochas le Dia: Thanks be to God.

Uncensored

Unopened envelopes sitting on a table.
Thirteen years I've waited
for this opportunity
of unhindered and unhampered
opening for my eyes only
a letter.
No screw, no censor, no prying
into my life and privacy.
Just a small gesture
just a small signal of freedom
just what I've been waiting for.

After the Break

Facing inwards for a lifetime
I wanted to face out
to be part of what's wider
than the narrow corridor.
To experience, enjoy
participate in a life
that in this life is
permanently denied.
Now having been there
I face outward
wanting to face in
to regain that normality
of routine
to be part of where I am
not where I want to be.
Inward, outward, the wrench
has broken many a neck
and my particular struggle
is now to keep in check
the aspirations from the options
the future from the immediate
for I am where I am
and that is where
my duties lie.

Weightlifting

You carry a weight so long
it loses consequence.
It's like having big arms
or a huge head,
the body learns to cope with the load.
It's only when it is removed
you feel the instant benefits.
We carry weights, too.
We've had them so long
They've become forgotten. Mental weights
aggravating incrementally, bit by bit
but unlike the camel's back
the mind absorbs
strengthening as the load grows.
Each day's new problem
is only heavy for as long
as it takes to absorb it
with yesterday's
making room for tomorrow's.
Yet, forgotten or not
They're there, they exist
and on that day, that instant
when the turnstile spilled me out
I felt the load lift, unmassed
en masse.
Elation, andrenaline,
weightlifting.

Questioner

There is no salvation for a troubled soul
and that is the curse of eternal damnation,
that a soul, spirit, *anam*, inner sense of being
should remain uneasy.
That restless quest and questioning
that seeking after answers,
that infernal Why? amid a myriad
of routes to resolution
where every exit leads into another maze
and every clue another complex twist
and every arrow points, directs and guides
the pilgrim to confusion.

Where then, salvation?
Is it written in some golden book
that those who question are unworthy?
And only those whose passive…
aye, or impassive lives
are symbols of their faith?
That only those who doubt not,
question not, be not questioned in return?
For the only souls
who are untroubled
are the souls who are immune
to life and its mystery.
Number me among the questioners
not the silent mass, and someday I will say
I'll be damned for asking why
but I'll be damned if I don't.

Fall

The halo he wore was not his own
nor had he a hand in its making
it was placed there by others over time
nor had he a hand in its breaking,
but the day that it slipped from above him
he helplessly watched as it dangled
till it settled in place around his neck
then by virtue of piety he was strangled.

Rekindling

The last flicker of the candle
threw a reddish hue around the table
where we sat, barefaced in our sadness
at the passing of an era.
Thoughts of a solitude to follow
the pending departure
we raised no hope of a recovery
and a writer studied an obituary
while an organiser marshalled
the procession in his mind
and a bugler rehearsed the Last Post
that would sound farewell.

Premature, always too soon
to accept defeat we should have paused
and postponed the wake until the death
while we sat in gloom the flicker
had already cast its seed
which shot from place to place
invigorating, absorbing idle energy
at every bounce growing
until in an explosion of light
the rebirth occurred:
only the vanquished were vanquished
the courageous rose again
to live and fight another day.

On Love

Like a jealous husband
waking his wife from sleep
to ask for whom she smiles
amidst her dreams
and like a careful mother
clutching a child to her breast
showing love
at even a fleeting moment
and like a broken gate
sounding louder than the wind
which blows it
always louder, always heard.
I will be jealous, I will clutch
I will be heard
and you will know I am there
beside you every day.

On Friendship

A friend will lean on you for support
only if you can bear the load
beware that you don't expect of others
what you will not give of yourself
that the weight of worry you unburden
in times of need
is not placed on the shoulders
of one who is close to breaking.
A friend will not destroy you
but will be destroyed by you
if you are not a friend.

An Unwelcome Companion

The ringing in my ears
was so constant, ceaseless
that after a few days
I had to stop
and listen
to detect it.

You become so used
to a companion
you live with a pain eventually
and the throbbing noise, unreal yet loud, loud
became that companion
until I could only detect it
at those moments when I craved
the silence of its absence
when I longed
for the absence of its silence
at those numb seconds
it seemed to sense my will
and intensified
winning the contest
against conscious intent
for only in idle daydreaming
time wasting
was I able
to hear myself think.

Two Views of Prison

From where I was sitting
three days in prison
was a bargain
weighed against a fine
of one hundred and twenty pounds.
Time in prison
is almost meaningless
and three days
is a blip.
You'd wait longer on a letter
or the dentist
you'd spend longer
without seeing the sky
on a wet winter week.
My advice
was to spend the fine
enjoy the pounds
and in the pound
spend three fine days.

From where you sat
a father's instinct spoke
you told me
that if it had been yours
to choose
to pay a fine for him, for me
we'd never have seen
the inside of these walls.
Nothing replaces liberty
you said
No price is too high, you said
for a father to pay.

Making Sense

There was a strength
about his touch. My father's touch
although it was gentle on my arm,
withdrawing, then returning
as my mother watched the screw
watching him, watching me.
So close he could hear the words
but not so close to hear
the tone, the reassurance
the bond in the voices
between us.
We drank the coffee—
neither tasting nor smelling—
a ritual and a function
something to fill a pause
not an empty stomach
something to bring home near
something shared ...
the real sharing
was in the three of us
sitting there, close
together, easy,
making sense of each other.

The Old Stock

I saw three loyalists today
and seeing them I saw
that all this bull
about a single culture *Ulster* people
is left null, and void
by jail.

The first, wearing a Celtic jersey
was so non-stereotypical
that the other two (unpractised
at reading the eyes, perhaps)
ignored him
as much as they ignored each other.
The second, grooming a moustache
that would have been in fashion
in the days of dash and rations
and the RAF in action
spoke to me.
God and Ulster knows why
perhaps the years have
mellowed his aversion
to my sort.
The third, sour, bitter, old now
clutching his status symbol
—a handicrafted picture
of an English soccer team—
sat silent, morose.
Armies and eras
years apart
the years wore nothing from his code.
Instead the lichen of new hatred
had enhanced the last of the old stock.

Horse Box

Bundled, hand-cuffed into the erect coffin
as narrow as a broad-shouldered man
as tall as a stooping Amazon
as deep as a casket
lit only by an opaque slot
with one upward-gazing slit
and walls, roof, floor and door padded
with stainless steel.
This is the mobile cell
this uncomfortable hell.

Horse Box II

Travelling, I should be seeing
fields of green, skies of blue
all the cliches that we use
describing views.
Instead, I tumble past
recording not the undulating hills
or meandering streams
but every jolt and bump and hurt
of every pothole
and the lurch and sway and swagger
of every bend.
While instead of the sweet breeze
perfumed with the growing flowers
sweeping through a window
I am nauseated by the sickly stench
of diesel fumes
seeping upwards through the floor
of this horse-box.

I spent a week back in Crumlin Road Prison amongst remand prisoners in the late 1980s when taking a case against the NIO over censorship and the ban on the Irish language. The poems which follow are from that period.

A New View

A room with a view
if I climb high enough
and wedge a book below the flap
of metal which caps the window.
It's worth the trouble
I can look beyond the jail
for the first time.
I can see the majesty of a spire
red upon black stone
and the straight ridge
of a street of houses
and the lushness of a tree.
If it was my city I would cry
instead I enjoy the view
of an untinned world.

Time Warp

Back at the coalface
of naked sectarian hate.
It's twelve years' past
since I was last in this pit
but the remarks they call
are much the same:

Hi Provo, your ma is this,
your da is that,
your sister is the other.
We silently sit
It's not worth the bother
of climbing up to a window
to shout the same crap back.
The sign of a hood
is a hoarse throat,
foaming mouth,
and an empty head
whose ears, it appears, have no use
beyond
listening to the sound
of his own voice.

Among New Comrades

Fleeting meetings
among a group of men
whose interests now are different
from what they were
two weeks or months ago
or will be two months hence.
The big problem of the day
is whether a man should shave
or shower first.
People have fought wars over less
and so we go slow
s l o w, s l o w
And the questions
of what it's like below
with me only hoping
I'm giving
the right answer
but not too
quickly.

Charged Batteries

The amazing thing is
that I'm back now in the blocks
almost as long
as I was away, up there.
And yet from the space
of those four short days
I've retained enough memories
to keep me in talk
for weeks.
From the space of a couple of hours
in court
enough to keep me relating
for days.
Every step, every stair tread,
every brick, every face,
every cell, every screw,
every visit, every minute
filling my mind anew
giving the flush of adrenalin
recharging batteries
and even in losing
finding gains
before returning, tired
yet re-energised
to the blocks again.

Cross Examination

Like spiders knitting bureaucratic webs
of rules and regulations
criss-crossing in anticipation of my head
as the first oblation
spinning civil servants setting out the traps
of un-baited snares
satisfied to catch by chance, these satraps
ambush only the unaware
Not content with dark corners remote from view
they spin in full daylight
and, in search of bright new paths for the few
who fall are caught tight.
Once, twice, I felt the gentle tug
of the subtle nettings hold
but broken free, grateful, never smug
the dummy never sold.
The art, if art there is, to pull away
directly avoiding contest;
volte-face in the most deliberate way
ensures I come out best
because to tangle, to wrangle, to debate
is to let the bonds unfold
meshing to the centre of the web, a grim fate
awaits me there I'm told.

Prowlers

Before you close your eyes to sleep tonight
be careful, check, scan around, be ready
for the late night-early morning knock
has returned. The unannounced caller
the disrupter of sleep
and sweet dreams is back
to invade your privacy, your cell,
your body, your slumber,
trying to catch you inert
instead of alert.
Tonight be wary, sleep lightly
for the prowler doesn't sleep at all.

AUDIO FILES

 Gerry Adams reads 'Building Trouble'

 Christy Moore reads 'Easter 1982'

 Séanna Breathnach reads 'Mackies Men'

 Lachlan Whalen reads 'Vigil'

Rosie McCorley reads 'Point Number Three'

Barra Mac Giolla Dhuibh reads 'Multi-tone Monotone'

Alison Mac Cormaic reads 'A Night Sound and a Thought'

James Doran reads 'Acquaintance Renewed'

Jim Ward reads 'A Dog's Life'

Danny Morrison reads 'No News, Good News'

Martina Anderson reads 'Ghosts of Armagh Gaol'

Raymond McCartney reads 'Easter 1989'

Vincent Higgins reads 'Inhospitality'

Verena Commins reads 'The First Official Language'

Rita Ann Higgins reads 'Mental Playground'

Laurence McKeown reads 'Language and Pain'

Liadán Nic Cormaic reads 'A Reflection Across the Yard'

Colm Scullion reads 'My Gain, Your Loss'

Paula McFetridge reads 'Ground Level'

Máiréad Farrell and Eoin Ó Broin read 'Reading between the lines in Gibraltar'

Brendan McFarlane reads 'Biko'

Pat Sheehan reads 'Mandelamandla'

Ali Mac Aindreasa reads 'The Face of Christ'

Eoghan Mac Cormaic reads 'On My First Bike'

 Jenny Meegan reads 'Fringe Life'

 Malachaí Mac Cormaic reads 'Teacher'

 Toiréasa Ferris reads 'Cnoc na gCróga'

 Diarmuid de Faoite reads 'The Year of the Frog'

 Tony Doherty reads 'Marchers'

 Gerry Kelly reads 'Camilo Torres'

 Mitchel McLaughlin reads 'Creggan Hill'

 Sarah McLaughlin reads 'The Hunter and the Hunted'

 Órlaith Mac Eoin Manus reads 'Uncensored'

 Lucilita Bhreatnach reads 'Rekindling'

Eibhlín Nic Cormaic reads 'Horse-Box II'

Máiridh Nic Cormaic reads 'A New View'

Other books by Greenisland Press

  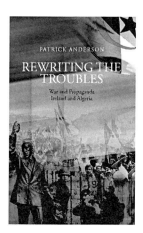

Free Statism & The Good Old IRA by Danny Morrison, published January 2022

Danny Morrison challenges Fianna Fáil, Fine Gael and the Irish establishment over their attitude to partition and how the closer conditions are met for a border referendum—which could have a profound effect on Ireland's constitutional future—the further they retreat from it.

'… apart from being a full-frontal assault on the sanctimony of Fine Gael and Fianna Fáil, [*Free Statism*] opens the door to a much more profound debate about the state they created while turning their backs on the six counties that they abandoned to Unionist rule.'

Roy Greenslade

Curious Journey—The IRA and Cumann na mBan, 1916-1923 by Timothy O'Grady and Kenneth Griffith, published July 2022.

Timothy O'Grady and the late Kenneth Griffith spoke at length to nine IRA and Cumann na mBan elderly veterans of the Rising through the Civil War period for a television film that was later banned. They turned it into a book first published in 1982, which has been revised by Timothy O'Grady to coincide with the centenary of the Treaty and Civil War.

'superb insight into the founding of the Irish nation ... This is Irish history at its best, told by the men and women who lived it.'

Irish Post

Rewriting the Troubles—War and Propaganda, Ireland and Algeria by Dr Patrick Anderson, published August 2022.

In this timely and meticulously researched book Anderson compares and contrasts Algeria's anti-colonial struggle with the republican campaign to dismantle Britain's colonial legacy. With devastating effect, he dissects the British media's widely differing portrayals of remarkably similar conflicts over the same constitutional issue. 'Unionists, including academics, have been aware of the striking analogies between Algeria and the north for decades: they all reject the uncanny similarities as dangerous... It's easy to see why... Accepting any analogy or similarity means accepting that the north is illegal, a temporary arrangement, and that Britain will eventually leave Ireland as the French did Algeria.'

Dr Brian Feeney, *Irish News*